T0277848

BALLPARK GREATS

PRO BASEBALL'S BEST PLAYERS

CHRISTIAN YELICH

DONALD PARKER

BALLPARK GREATS

PRO BASEBALL'S BEST PLAYERS

CHRISTIAN YELICH

JUSTIN VERLANDER

MAX SCHERZER

MIKE TROUT

NOLAN ARENADO

BALLPARK GREATS

PRO BASEBALL'S BEST PLAYERS

CHRISTIAN YELICH

DONALD PARKER

MASON CREST

PHILADELPHIA

MIAMI

Mason Crest
450 Parkway Drive, Suite D
Broomall, Pennsylvania 19008
(866) MCP-BOOK (toll-free)
www.masoncrest.com

First printing
9 8 7 6 5 4 3 2 1

ISBN (hardback) 978-1-4222-4441-8
ISBN (series) 978-1-4222-4434-0
ISBN (ebook) 978-1-4222-7376-0

Library of Congress Cataloging-in-Publication Data

Names: Parker, Donald, author.
Title: Christian Yelich / Donald Parker.
Description: Broomall : Mason Crest, [2020] | Series: Ballpark greats: pro
   baseball's best players | Includes bibliographical references and index.
Identifiers: LCCN 2019038682 | ISBN 9781422244418 (hardback) |
   ISBN 9781422273760 (ebook)
Subjects: LCSH: Yelich, Christian, 1991—Juvenile literature. | Baseball
   players—United States—Biography—Juvenile literature.
Classification: LCC GV865.Y43 P37 2020 | DDC 796.357092 [B]—dc23
LC record available at https://lccn.loc.gov/2019038682

Developed and Produced by National Highlights Inc.
Editor: Andrew Luke
Production: Crafted Content LLC

QR CODES AND LINKS TO THIRD-PARTY CONTENT

CONTENTS

KEY ICONS TO LOOK FOR:

 Words to Understand: These words with their easy-to-understand definitions will increase the reader's understanding of the text while building vocabulary skills.

 Sidebars: This boxed material within the main text allows readers to build knowledge, gain insights, explore possibilities, and broaden their perspectives by weaving together additional information to provide realistic and holistic perspectives.

 Educational Videos: Readers can view videos by scanning our QR codes, providing them with additional educational content to supplement the text. Examples include news coverage, moments in history, speeches, iconic sports moments, and much more!

 Text-Dependent Questions: These questions send the reader back to the text for more careful attention to the evidence presented there.

 Research Projects: Readers are pointed toward areas of further inquiry connected to each chapter. Suggestions are provided for projects that encourage deeper research and analysis.

 Series Glossary of Key Terms: This back-of-the-book glossary contains terminology used throughout this series. Words found here increase the reader's ability to read and comprehend higher-level books and articles in this field.

WORDS TO UNDERSTAND

catalyst: an agent that provokes or speeds significant change or ac

dividends: a return or reward arising as a consequence, effect, or conclusion of something

rival: one striving for competitive advantage

CHAPTER 1

GREATEST MOMENTS

CHRISTIAN YELICH'S MLB CAREER

Christian Yelich has quickly developed into one of the best hitters in all of Major League Baseball (MLB). The Florida Marlins drafted him with their first pick in the 2010 draft, and after several years of being a role player, he has emerged as a budding superstar. Yelich began showing flashes of his potential greatness in the 2016 MLB season. It was in that season that he finished in double digits in home runs (21), had 98 runs batted in (RBI), scored 78 runs, and posted a .298 batting average. He continued to develop into a consistent player for the Marlins but never found his star on a team with players like Christian Colon, J. T. Realmuto, and future 2017 National League (NL) MVP Giancarlo Stanton who, like Yelich, left the Marlins in 2018 (Stanton went to the New York Yankees).

Yelich finalized a nearly $50 million deal with the Marlins to begin the 2015 season. An injury to his back sidelined him for two weeks and a slow start at the plate resulted in his sharing time in the field. He never quite found his footing as a starter. In fact, he finished the 2015 season with the league's highest ground ball percentage of all hitters at 62.5 percent but, remarkably, the lowest fly ball percentage at 15 percent. He continued sharing his time in the field and eventually was part of a four-player trade with the Milwaukee Brewers in January 2018. The Marlins picked up two prospects in the deal, thought to be in their favor, whereas the Brewers received just Yelich. What the Brewers ultimately ended up getting, however, was a two-time All-Star, league Most Valuable Player (MVP), and the **catalyst** needed to take the team back to the playoffs.

Yelich has developed into one of the best players in the league. He went from sharing time in a crowded outfield for a Marlins team with a losing record to a playoff contender and team in Milwaukee that missed the 2018 World Series by one game. He has even fixed his low fly ball problem from 2015, launching 36 home runs in 2018 and being one of the league's leaders in the same category in 2019 (hitting 44). He has not changed his approach to the game, but he has clearly risen from contributor to star.

GREATEST CAREER MOMENTS

HERE IS A LIST OF SOME OF YELICH'S CAREER FIRSTS AND GREATEST ACHIEVEMENTS DURING HIS TIME IN MLB:

REACHES 1,000TH CAREER HITS MILESTONE

Since joining the Milwaukee Brewers in 2018, Yelich has reached several milestones in his career. One of those milestones was becoming a member of the 1,000 hits club. He joined a group of 1,340 other MLB players to hit this mark in a game against the Pittsburgh Pirates on June 30, 2019. Yelich hit a ball down the left field line in the bottom of the third inning off Pirates starting pitcher Steven Brault. The resulting double was good enough to put him in the club. He became the 11th Brewer to record 1,000 hits in a career (1,031) and now ranks number 10 just above former catcher Charlie Moore, who had 1,029 hits.

Yelich hits an opposite-field double off Pittsburgh pitcher Steven Brault in the third inning of a June 30, 2019, game for his 1,000th career major league hit.

HITS HIS 100TH CAREER HOME RUN

The hits kept coming for Yelich in 2019. Part of his more than 1,000 career MLB hits include 131 career home runs, 72 of which came while wearing his Milwaukee uniform. Facing division foes Chicago Cubs in an early-season April matchup, Yelich drove the first pitch of pitcher Kyle Hendricks 408 feet (124.4 m) over the right centerfield fence for a two-run home run. The runs were enough to lead the Brew Crew to a 4–2 victory. The home run marked the 100th home run in his young career. In the 2019 season, Yelich would go on to become just the 10th MLB player to ever hit at least 40 home runs and steal at least 30 bases in a season.

He hit his 100th career home run, and his first in a Milwaukee Brewers' uniform, in game 3 of a series against division rival, Chicago Cubs.

FIRST MLB ALL-STAR GAME START

Trading for Yelich in 2018 paid immediate **dividends** for Milwaukee, because he was a superstar in the making. He was named to his first All-Star squad in 2018. Yelich's efforts to start the 2019 campaign once again earned him recognition as one of the best players in the National League. This time, the recognition came from the fans, as he was voted to start the All-Star game for the first time. In just his second appearance, Yelich was second overall in the fan vote (behind former American League [AL] MVP Mike Trout of the Los Angeles Angels). Trout got 993,857 votes compared to Yelich's NL-leading 930,577.

Yelich was named to his second career MLB All-Star game in consecutive years as a member of the Milwaukee Brewers. 2019 marked the first time in his career that he was named to the starting lineup.

YELICH EARNS NL MVP HONORS

Batting .326, hitting 36 home runs, scoring 118 runs, and helping the Milwaukee Brewers win the National League Central Division (and make it all the way to the league's championship game) was enough to help Yelich earn 2018 NL MVP honors. He beat out Chicago Cubs infielder Javier Baez for the award. Yelich received all but one of the 30 first-place votes, with the other vote going to eventual NL Cy Young Award winner Jacob deGrom of the New York Mets. Along with leading the league in hitting, Yelich was also tops in slugging, on-base plus slugging percentage and total bases, setting career highs for all.

Yelich (NL) and Mookie Betts of the Boston Red Sox (AL) earned their respective league's Most Valuable Player awards for the 2018 MLB season.

YELICH GOES A PERFECT 6-FOR-6 AND HITS FOR THE CYCLE

In an August 29, 2018, road game against the Cincinnati Reds, Yelich recorded six hits. Three went for singles, along with one each for a double, triple, and a home run. He also ended up scoring twice and knocking in three runs. Yelich's effort helped lead the Brewers to a much-needed 13–12, 10-inning win against the Reds to keep pace with the Chicago Cubs for the overall division lead. This game marked the first time in his career that he hit for the cycle—hitting a single, a double, a triple, and a home run in the same game. Less than three weeks later, Yelich hit for the cycle again, also against the Reds.

He is the fifth player in MLB history to record two cycles in the same season, and the first to do so against the same opponent.

Highlights of Yelich's first career game in which he hit for the cycle as the Brewers beat division foe Cincinnati 13–12 in extra innings.

WON GOLD GLOVE AWARD

Yelich received a Gold Glove Award in the 2014 season while playing left field for the Miami Marlins. The award, which honors the best fielders by position in their respective leagues, recognizes a player's defensive skills. His 2014 season, played mostly in left field (138 of 144 games played in 2014 for the Marlins), yielded an overall fielding percentage of 0.993. This is near perfect play. Yelich committed only two fielding errors, one in left and one in center field that season. He had 271 putouts over 279 defensive chances. He also chipped in with eight outfield assists, throwing runners out from all three outfield positions.

Yelich won his first Gold Glove Award as a member of the Miami Marlins in the 2014 MLB season.

WON NATIONAL LEAGUE BATTING TITLE

Winning the batting title in 2018 helped raise Yelich's profile among baseball journalists who cast their votes for MVP. How did he win the title? By ripping 187 hits for a .326 batting average, the best in the National League for 2018. He also led the National League with a 0.598 slugging percentage and reached base (including walks) just over 40 percent of the time. These numbers made him a dreaded hitter for National League pitchers to face and was one of the factors that contributed to his winning the title. In fact, Yelich fell just two home runs and one RBI short of becoming the first player since 1967 to win the Triple Crown. In the NL, no player has led the league in hitting, home runs and RBI since the Cardinal's Joe "Ducky" Medwick in 1937.

Yelich's 3-for-4 effort in an October 1, 2018, matchup against the Chicago Cubs for the National League Central Division title earned him the NL Batting Title with a season-ending 0.326 average.

WON SILVER SLUGGER AWARD

In addition to winning a Golden Glove Award while in a Marlins uniform (2014), Yelich won the first of three Silver Slugger Awards also while in Miami in 2016 (he also won the Silver Slugger award in each of 2018 and 2019 with Milwaukee). Yelich had a breakout year in 2016, hitting 21 home runs for the Marlins as well as posting a .298 batting average and batting in 98 runs. His HR and RBI totals in 2016 were both career highs for him at the time and boosted his stock as a player to watch. Yelich's .483 slugging percentage and .376 on-base percentage were also career highs at the time. Another career high that the voters luckily did not hold against him was his 138 strikeouts.

Yelich, speaking moments before the start of an April 12, 2017, game against the Atlanta Braves, discusses how honored he feels winning the Silver Slugger Award in 2016.

Yelich's career was filled with great moments through his first seven seasons.

TEXT-DEPENDENT QUESTIONS

1. Against what team did Yelich earn his 1,000th career hit? Who was the opposing pitcher?
2. How many Gold Glove Awards has he won? How many Silver Slugger Awards has he won in his career?
3. How many All-Star games has Yelich been named to? What year did he start an All-Star game?

RESEARCH PROJECT

Yelich is one of four Milwaukee Brewers players to be honored with the league's Most Valuable Player award. Yelich's teammate Ryan Braun won the NL award in 2011. Hall of Fame shortstop and center fielder Robin Yount won the American League MVP award twice, in 1982 and 1989, and Yount's teammate, Hall of Fame reliever Rollie Fingers, won both the AL MVP and Cy Young Awards in 1981 (the Brewers were an American League team from 1969 until 1996). Look at the current players in Major League Baseball. How many active MVP winners play on a team with another MVP winner? Name the players, the team they play together for, when they won the award, and the team each played for when they received their MVP award (if different from their current team).

WORDS TO UNDERSTAND

adept: thoroughly advanced in an art, occupation, or branch of knowledge

affiliate: a close associate

landscape: the natural features of the land surface in a region

CHAPTER 2

THE ROAD TO THE TOP

YELICH'S PLAYER PERFORMANCE

Christian Stephen Yelich was born on December 5, 1991, in the city of Thousand Oaks, California. Thousand Oaks, with a population of nearly 130,000 residents, is located in the northwest corner of the Greater Los Angeles area. The city is a mere 40 miles (64 km) from downtown Los Angeles. It is named for the many oak trees that make up the city's **landscape**. The city is the home and birthplace of several notable athletes and performers, including Aaron Donald and Jared Goff of the NFL's Los Angeles Rams; former NHL superstar and Hockey Hall of Famer Wayne Gretzky; talk show host Ellen DeGeneres; and actor Kurt Russell, a 1969 graduate of Thousand Oaks High School, who briefly played minor league baseball from 1971–1973 before choosing a career in film.

Yelich developed a love for the game of baseball very early in life. He played all four years of varsity-level baseball while attending Westlake High School (Nickname: Warriors) in his hometown of Thousand Oaks. Yelich's career batting average in high school of .416 made him a top 100 high school prospect

Ultramodern Marlins Park opened in Miami the year before Yelich was called up.

and earned him All-American honors. He was as **adept** in the field with his glove but not in the outfield, where he plays for the Milwaukee Brewers. Yelich was a starting third and first baseman for his Warriors team.

Yelich, who graduated from Westlake in 2010, is six feet three inches (1.93 m) and 195 pounds (88 kg). His ability to hit the ball with power and play the infield was enough for recruiters from the University of Miami of the Atlantic Coast Conference (ACC) to offer him a scholarship to play college baseball. The Florida Marlins baseball team (which would change its name to Miami Marlins the next year) made a more tempting offer, however. Florida selected Yelich in the first round of the 2010 amateur draft. Yelich waited until the last moment to accept the Marlins offer and a $1.7 million signing bonus to play professional baseball.

ATHLETIC ACCOMPLISHMENTS

HIGH SCHOOL

Yelich was a high school freshman in 2006. He had played in several Little Leagues and youth leagues as a kid growing up in Thousand Oaks, all while admiring the play of his favorite major league team, the Los Angeles Dodgers. He came to Westlake, a national high school baseball powerhouse, ready to learn the fundamentals of the game and develop the skills that he would need to make it to the next level.

Yelich grew up in Southern California rooting for the Mike Piazza–led LA Dodgers.

CHRISTIAN YELICH
DRAFT DAY

The Florida Marlins selected Yelich with the 23rd pick in the first round of the 2010 amateur baseball draft.

The 2010 draft consisted of 50 rounds. A total of 1,525 players were selected. It was held June 7–9, 2010, at the home of MLB Network located in Secaucus, New Jersey.

Bryce Harper, an outfielder at the University of Southern Nevada, was the first overall selection in the 2010 draft, taken by the Washington Nationals. He was the second consecutive number-one selection for the Nationals, who selected pitcher Stephen Strasburg in the 2009 amateur draft out of San Diego State University.

2010 DRAFT DAY
SIGNIFICANT ACCOUNTS

- Three players selected in the draft went on to play in the NFL. They are Russell Wilson (QB, Seattle Seahawks), selected in the fourth round (140th pick) by the Colorado Rockies; Blake Bell (TE, Kansas City Chiefs), selected in the 43rd round (1,303rd pick); and Golden Tate (WR, New York Giants), selected in the 50th round (1,518th pick). Wilson and Tate were members of the Seahawk's 2014 Super Bowl XLVIII championship team.

- Yelich was the fifth outfielder selected in the first round. The most commonly selected position in the first round was pitcher—14 pitchers were drafted in the first round.

- In the 31st round, the Oakland Athletics drafted outfielder Aaron Judge, but he did not sign with the A's, opting to go to Fresno State instead. In 2013, he went back to the draft and was the first-round pick of the New York Yankees. Judge would go on to win the 2017 AL Rookie of the Year award after hitting a league-best and MLB-rookie-record 52 home runs.

- In the 18th round, the Toronto Blue Jays picked third baseman Kris Bryant, but he chose to play at the University of San Diego instead. Like Judge, he reentered the draft in 2013 and was taken in the first round, second overall, by the Chicago Cubs. Bryant won the 2016 NL MVP award and led the Cubs to the 2016 World Series championship.

- Future All-Star outfielder Corey Dickerson was drafted in the eighth round (260th overall) by Colorado.

- Of the 32 first round picks, 17 were used to select high school seniors. The other 15 picks went for National Collegiate Athletic Association players.

Yelich was a starter on the Warriors varsity team as a freshman, playing the infield corners at either first or third base. He wielded a pretty decent bat, posting a batting average of .451 and hitting nine home runs. Yelich played in 28 games in his sophomore season at Westlake. He made 94 plate appearances, scoring 31 times while hitting five home runs and driving in 29 runs. He struck out only six times for a batting average of .489.

Yelich continued his success as a high school player, hitting .341 with six home runs in his junior season in 2009. He scored 30 runs for the Warriors and collected 23 RBI and 31 hits (as well as 52 total bases). Yelich finished his high school career in 2010 with a total of 139 hits, a batting average of .416, and 20 home runs.

Yelich's numbers while playing for the Westlake High School Warriors from 2007–2010 were

Year	G	AB	R	H	2B	3B	HR	RBI	SB	BB	SO	BA
2006–07 (FR)	28	82	41	37	14	2	9	25	28	30	9	0.451
2007–08 (SO)	28	94	31	46	8	3	5	29	23	16	6	0.489
2008–09 (JR)	29	91	30	31	6	0	6	23	12	21	24	0.341
2009–10 (SR)	25	67	9	25	5	1	0	12	2	8	16	0.373
TOTALS	110	334	111	139	33	6	20	89	65	75	55	0.416

Yelich was a consistent starter throughout his four-year high school career at Westlake High. His numbers made him a highly regarded prospect for both college and MLB scouts. He left high school in fine position to become a rising star at whatever next level he chose to play.

HIGH SCHOOL ALL-AMERICAN

Yelich developed into a top major league prospect while playing for the Westlake High School (Thousand Oaks, California) Warriors. He played in 110 games as an infielder (first and third base). He had a .416 batting average over his four years, hitting 20 home runs with an on-base percentage of .532 (meaning he reached base more than half the times he appeared at the plate). Yelich's numbers were good enough for him to be named second-team All-American by *Baseball America* and *MaxPreps*. It was quite an accomplishment for the young Yelich, who finished behind first-team infielders Manny Machado (San Diego Padres) and Kris Bryant of the Chicago Cubs.

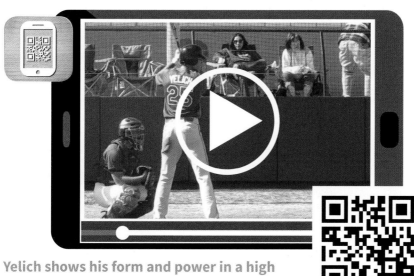

Yelich shows his form and power in a high school matchup versus Bishop Gorman High School (Gaels) in Las Vegas in 2010. This home run was one of the many reasons he was named a high school All-American.

2010 AMATEUR BASEBALL DRAFT

At the 2010 amateur baseball draft, 1,525 players were drafted in 50 rounds of selections. The top player taken in the draft was OF Bryce Harper from Southern Nevada University, selected by the Washington Nationals. (Harper signed with the Philadelphia Phillies as a free agent at the start of the 2019 MLB season.) Of the 50 players selected in the first round of the draft, 14 were on active MLB rosters as of the start of the 2019 season.

Bryce Harper was the number-one overall pick of the 2010 amateur draft.

The Florida Marlins selected Yelich out of high school with the 23rd overall pick. He was passed over for other far less successful outfielders like Michael Choice (number 10 to Oakland) and Jake Skole (number 15 to Texas).

MINOR LEAGUE RESULTS

Yelich spent his first four seasons after signing with the Marlins (and receiving a $1.7 million signing bonus) in the club's minor league system. Before joining the Marlins as a regular major league player in 2013,

In 2012, Yelich played 106 games for the Marlins' Class A-Advanced affiliate Jupiter Hammerheads of the Florida State league.

elich hit .288 in the big eagues, while splitting his 013 season between Miami nd minor league affiliates n Jacksonville and Jupiter.

he made stops played with Miami **affiliates** in Greensboro, North Carolina; Jupiter, Florida; Phoenix; and New Orleans. Yelich hit 37 home runs, 179 RBI, scored 211 runs, and had a batting average of .311.

Yelich's results in the minor leagues were

Year	Team/Class	G	AB	R	H	2B	3B	HR	RBI	SB	BB	SO	BA
2010	Greensboro (A)	6	23	2	8	2	0	0	2	0	1	6	0.348
2010	Marlins (Rk)	6	24	3	9	1	1	0	3	1	2	7	0.375
2011	Greensboro (A)	122	461	73	144	32	1	15	77	32	55	102	0.312
2012	Jupiter (A+)	106	397	76	131	29	5	12	48	20	49	85	0.330
2012	Marlins (Rk)	1	4	0	1	0	0	0	0	0	0	0	0.250
2012	Phoenix (Fall)	25	93	13	28	6	1	0	11	3	5	17	0.301
2013	Jacksonville (AA)	49	193	33	54	13	6	7	29	5	26	52	0.280
2013	Jupiter (A+)	7	26	3	6	0	0	2	4	0	4	8	0.231
2013	Marlins (Rk)	5	17	2	5	0	1	0	0	0	1	5	0.294
2014	New Orleans (AAA)	2	9	2	1	0	0	1	4	0	0	5	0.111
2014	Jupiter (A+)	2	6	2	2	0	0	0	1	1	1	1	0.333
2015	Jupiter (A+)	3	9	2	3	1	0	0	0	1	1	3	0.333
TOTALS		334	1262	211	392	84	15	37	179	63	145	291	0.311

TEXT-DEPENDENT QUESTIONS

1. Where did Yelich attend high school? What years did he attend high school?

2. What honors did he earn playing baseball in high school?

3. What was Yelich's batting average in his freshman year of high school? How many total home runs did he hit in high school?

RESEARCH PROJECT

Yelich was a second-team All-American in high school. He was honored as an infielder alongside future MLB stars Kris Bryant of the Chicago Cubs and Manny Machado of the San Diego Padres. These three players have accounted for 460 home runs, 2,908 hits, 1,611 runs, 1,443 RBI, and a batting average of 0.289. The trio also appeared in a total of nine All-Star games, won two NL MVP awards (one each for Yelich and Bryant), three Gold Glove Awards, and a Rookie of the Year Award for Kris Bryant in 2015. Looking at the high school All-American baseball players since 2000, list another trio of current MLB players who have as a group hit at least 400 home runs, 3,000 hits, and posted a batting average at or near .300, as well as have won multiple MLB awards (including MVP, Rookie of the Year and Cy Young Awards).

WORDS TO UNDERSTAND

confine: something (such as borders or walls) that encloses

inductee: one who is admitted as a member

platoon: to play (one player) alternately with another player in the same position

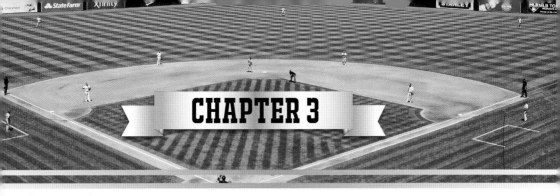

CHAPTER 3

ON THE DIAMOND

ACCOMPLISHMENTS ON THE FIELD

Yelich was more than ready for the challenge of playing at the big-league level when the Marlins brought him up from the minors for his first game on June 23, 2013. He has risen from a **platoon** player to an everyday starter, All-Star, and MVP winner.

Since Yelich played his first MLB game in 2013, he has been named

- Five-time MLB National League Player of the Week
- September 2018 MLB National League Player of the Month

Additionally, Yelich has won a Gold Glove award as a left fielder with the Miami Marlins in 2014 and three Silver Slugger Awards, the first in 2016 with the Marlins and the others as a member of the Milwaukee Brewers in 2018 and 2019. His on-base plus slugging percentage of 1.000 in 2018 led all National League hitters, as did his .598 slugging percentage in that season.

Other recognitions that Yelich has received as a result of his on-the-field performance include

- Three-time Silver Slugger Award Winner (2016, 2018, 2019)
- Two-time NL All-Star, (2018–2019)
- Recipient of the National League Hank Aaron Award in 2018
- Winner of the National League Most Valuable Player Award in 2018
- Winner of the National League hitting title in 2018 (.326 batting average)

CAREER TOTALS

Yelich has put up some impressive numbers as a player since his first game in 2013 for the Miami Marlins. His statistics have been even greater since he

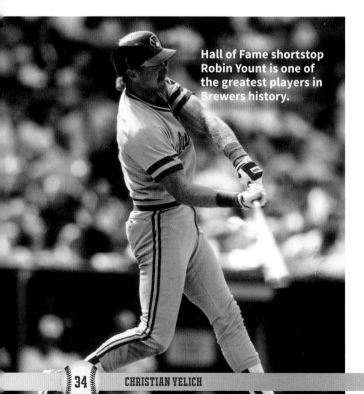

Hall of Fame shortstop Robin Yount is one of the greatest players in Brewers history.

was traded to the Milwaukee Brewers in 2018, which put him on track to becoming one of the greatest players to wear a Brewers uniform, along with names such as Paul Molitor, Hall of Fame **inductee** Robin Yount, Rollie Fingers, and others. He has developed into a consistent and feared power hitter, launching home runs almost

CHRISTIAN YELICH
Milwaukee Brewers
CAREER STATS

GP	BA	R	H	HR	RBI
920	.301	587	1067	139	500

OUTFIELD

- Date of birth: December 5, 1991

- Height: Six feet three inches (1.90 m), Weight: Approx. 195 pounds (88 kg)

- Two-time National League All-Star (2018, 2019)

- 2014 Gold Glove winner (outfield)

- Three-time Silver Slugger Award winner (2016, 2018, 2019)

- 2018 National League batting champion

- Hit for the cycle twice in his career

- 2018 Hank Aaron Award winner as best hitter in the National League

- Led National League in total bases (2018)

- Led National League in slugging (2018)

at will and hitting 55 percent of his career homers in less than two years in a Brewers uniform.

Here are the career and playoff game numbers Yelich has put up in his career to date.

Year	Team	G	AB	R	H	2B	3B	HR	RBI	SB	BB	SO	BA
2013	Miami	62	240	34	69	12	1	4	16	10	31	66	0.288
2014	Miami	144	582	94	165	30	6	9	54	21	70	137	0.284
2015	Miami	126	476	63	143	30	2	7	44	16	47	101	0.300
2016	Miami	155	578	78	172	38	3	21	98	9	72	138	0.298
2017	Miami	156	602	100	170	36	2	18	81	16	80	137	0.282
2018	Milwaukee	147	574	118	187	34	7	36	110	22	68	135	0.326
2019	Milwaukee	130	489	100	161	29	3	44	97	30	80	118	0.329
TOTALS		889	3427	565	1031	202	24	131	484	117	427	800	0.301

Bold indicates seasons where Yelich led the National League in that statistical category.

PLAYOFF TOTALS

Yelich has played in a total of 10 playoff games in his career, all with the Milwaukee Brewers. He reached the playoffs for the first time in his career in 2018, helping the Brewers win the National League Central Division in a one-game sudden-death regular season game against the rival Chicago Cubs.

Yelich has had far better success at the plate in the regular season versus in the playoffs.

For that game, played October 1, 2018, Yelich went 3-for-4 with an RBI that helped lead Milwaukee to a 3–1 division-clinching victory.

Yelich's efforts helped the Brewers reach the National League Division Series against the Colorado Rockies (who beat the Cubs in the one-game wildcard matchup). His 2-for-8 hitting in the series included a single and a home run, as well as scoring four times as the Crew beat the Rockies in three straight games. This helped Yelich reach his first league championship series, a matchup against the Los Angeles Dodgers. He played in seven games, collecting five hits, a double, and home run. His first career championship series appearance resulted in a loss but gave him a taste of things to come in his career.

Here are the totals Yelich has recorded in his 10-game playoff history, which includes an overall .194 batting average, seven hits, a double, two home runs, and two stolen bases.

Year	Series	Opp		G	AB	R	H	2B	3B	HR	RBI	SB	BB	SO	BA
2018	NLDS	COL	W	3	8	4	2	0	0	1	2	2	6	0	0.250
2018	NLCS	LAD	L	7	28	3	5	1	0	1	1	0	5	7	0.179
TOTALS				10	36	7	7	1	0	2	3	2	11	7	0.194

The move from sunny Florida to the colder **confines** of Milwaukee, Wisconsin, has done wonders for Yelich's prospects as a player. His game has risen to the level of greatness in a very short period—less than two seasons. Yelich saw playoff action for the first time in 2018, making it to within one game of the World Series. The National League Championship series that he appeared in was against the Los Angeles Dodgers, a team that Yelich grew up admiring as a kid growing up in Thousand Oaks, California. Having the ability to face his childhood team as a player was certainly a highpoint of his career.

Miller Park in Milwaukee became Yelich's new home stadium in 2018.

MVP STATE

Due to its milk and cheese production, some know the state of Wisconsin as the Dairy State. It may want to consider changing its name to the "MVP State." Yelich became the fourth player in Milwaukee Brewers history to win the MVP award, joining Hall of Fame players Rollie Fingers (1981) and Robin Yount (twice, in 1982 and 1989) and current teammate Ryan Braun (2011). Additionally, he joins the list of active Wisconsin-based pro player MVPs: Green Bay Packers quarterback Aaron Rodgers, a two-time NFL MVP in 2011 and 2014, and 2018–2019 Milwaukee Bucks forward and NBA MVP Giannis Antetokounmpo.

Wisconsin sports trio of MVPs, Green Bay Packers Aaron Rodgers and Brewers Ryan Braun and Christian Yelich, give advice to the newest member of the state's MVP club, Milwaukee Bucks star Giannis Antetokounmpo.

Primarily a left fielder in Miami, Yelich moved to right field with Milwaukee.

BASIC STATISTICS FOR YELICH

How well has Yelich developed as a player? Certainly, his numbers in terms of hits, home runs, RBI, and runs scored have all gone up since he joined the Brewers. He has become regarded as one of the best pure hitters in the game, with the ability to change the nature of a game instantly. He hits line drives as well as home runs and can make a pitcher nervous whenever he steps in the batter's box.

In five seasons with the Marlins, Yelich did not slug higher than .483, a number he far surpassed in both of his first two seasons in Milwaukee.

Three hitting statistics that are used to measure a hitter's ability, other than his batting average, are the following:

- *On-base percentage (OBP)*—a measurement of how often a player reaches base, which is calculated as the sum of hits, walks, and times a batter is hit by a pitch divided by the sum of the number of at bats, walks, time hit by a pitch, and sacrifice fly balls hit.
- *Slugging percentage (SLG)*—slugging percentage is an accumulation of the types of hits against at-bats. Each type of hit is given a factor, for example, a single is worth one point, a double is worth two, three points for a triple, and a home run is worth four. The sum of each hit divided by the number of at bats results in a player's slugging percentage.
- *On-base plus slugging percentage (OPS)*—the sum of on-base percentage plus slugging percentage.

Here is a look at Yelich's hitting statistics in the minor leagues, the regular season, and the 10 playoff games he saw action in during his 2018 MVP year.

Seven-time MVP Barry Bonds was Yelich's hitting coach with the Marlins in 2016.

MINOR LEAGUE
HITTING STATISTICS

Year	Team	LG/CLASS	OBP	SLG	OPS
2010	Greensboro	SoAtl/A	0.375	0.435	0.810
2010	Marlins	Gulf/Rk	0.423	0.500	0.923
2011	Greensboro	SoAtl/A	0.388	0.484	0.871
2012	Jupiter	FLSt/A+	0.404	0.519	0.922
2012	Marlins	Gulf/Rk	0.250	0.250	0.500
2012	Phoenix	AZFall/Fall	0.343	0.387	0.731
2013	Jacksonville	South/AA	0.365	0.518	0.883
2013	Jupiter	FLSt/A+	0.333	0.462	0.795
2013	Marlins	Gulf/Rk	0.333	0.412	0.745
2014	New Orleans	PCL/AAA	0.111	0.444	0.556
2014	Jupiter	FLSt/A+	0.429	0.333	0.762
2015	Jupiter	FLSt/A+	0.400	0.444	0.844
TOTALS			0.383	0.489	0.872

REGULAR SEASON MLB
HITTING STATISTICS

Year	Team	OBP	SLG	OPS
2013	Miami	0.370	0.396	0.766
2014	Miami	0.362	0.402	0.764
2015	Miami	0.366	0.416	0.782
2016	Miami	0.376	0.483	0.859
2017	Miami	0.369	0.439	0.807
2018	Milwaukee	0.402	0.598	1.000
2019	Milwaukee	0.429	0.671	1.100
TOTALS		0.381	0.488	0.870

MLB PLAYOFF
HITTING STATISTICS

Year	Series	OBP	SLG	OPS
2018	NLDS	0.571	0.625	1.196
2018	NLCS	0.303	0.321	0.624
TOTALS		0.383	0.389	0.772

TEXT-DEPENDENT QUESTIONS

1. What year was Yelich traded to the Milwaukee Brewers? What team traded Yelich to the Brewers?

2. What titles did Yelich earn in the 2018 season?

3. What does OPS stand for? How is it calculated? What does OBP stand for? How is it calculated?

RESEARCH PROJECT

Yelich was drafted 23rd overall by the Florida Marlins in the first round of the 2010 baseball amateur draft. Two other players drafted that year were Bryce Harper (first pick overall by the Washington Nationals), who joined the Philadelphia Phillies in 2019 as a free agent signing, and Manny Machado (third pick overall by the Baltimore Orioles), who went to San Diego via free agency in 2019. Looking at the hitting stats of these three stars, rank them in order of these categories: hits, home runs, runs, RBI, slugging percentage, OBP, and OPS.

WORDS TO UNDERSTAND

ambassador: an unofficial representative

campaign: a connected series of operations designed to bring about a particular result

phenomenal: extraordinary; remarkable

resurgence: a rising again into life, activity, or prominence

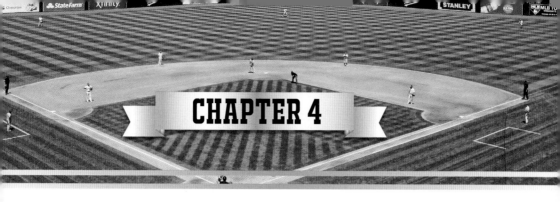

CHAPTER 4

WORDS COUNT

When the time comes to address the media before or after a game, players either retreat to the comfort of traditional phrases that avoid controversy (Cliché City), or they speak their mind with refreshing candor (Quote Machine).

Here are 10 quotes, compiled in part from the website BrainyQuote. com, with some insight as to the context of what Yelich is talking about or referencing:

> **"I think the biggest thing is just focusing on the day to day, your routine, not getting caught up in the future or the past and just being right there and focusing on what you have to do that day or that night to help your team win."**

Yelich had a **phenomenal** 2018 **campaign** in his first year in Milwaukee. He led the National League in batting average (.326), slugging percentage (.598), and on-base percentage plus slugging (1.000). His 36 home runs and 110 RBI

Yelich led the league in hitting, slugging, OPS, and total bases in his 2018 MVP season.

placed him among the league leaders in those categories. He was an important part of the Brewers' **resurgence** as a top team in the NL. Appearing in the National League Championship Series (NLCS) and winning the NL MVP award were the icing on the cake for him. It may be a cliché, but this quote shows recognition of his 2018 effort while also recognizing that his focus lies not in the past, but toward the future. This forward-thinking approach helps Yelich contribute to the team's success and winning ball games. **Rating: Cliché City**

"**I'm really thankful for the opportunity the Marlins gave me. They drafted me in 2010 and gave me a chance to play in the big leagues. I made lifelong friends there, and I've got a lot of great memories.**"

The Florida Marlins selected Yelich in the first round with the 23rd pick of the 2010 amateur draft. He spent the first eight seasons of his professional baseball career in the Marlins organization, the first three and a half in the minor leagues and the next four and a half as part of the big league lineup of the Marlins. Yelich recognizes that had it not been for the faith the Marlins had in him and their willingness to select him in the draft, he might not have had the chance not only to play, but to develop into one of the best players in all of Major League Baseball. Any ill will he may feel toward the team for trading him is masked in this clichéd quote, in which Yelich says he looks back on his time in Miami with great memories of the experiences he had and the relationships he developed with other players. **Rating: Cliché City**

> **"It's pretty ridiculous how nice people are in Milwaukee. It's like you're a member of everyone's family or something."**

Yelich joined the Milwaukee Brewers for the 2018 MLB season. Growing up in Thousand Oaks, California, and spending the first several years of his baseball career in Miami, he did not know what to expect when he was sent packing to the colder climate of Milwaukee, Wisconsin. He had few expectations as to what he would encounter when arriving from Florida but found himself pleasantly surprised by the warmth and friendliness of the team's fans and the city that adopted him as one of its own. The quote describes his feeling about the city and the team and the friendliness of everyone who has made him "one of the family." **Rating: Quote Machine**

> ## "It happens throughout the year where your swing feels better, or it feels worse; you feel good, you feel bad."

This is a clichéd reference to the ups and downs of a baseball season. Yelich is a consistent hitter, reaching base nearly 40 percent of the time in his career. He is both a contact hitter—meaning that he consistently puts the ball in play and rarely strikes out—and a power hitter, with 139 career home runs and a career slugging percentage of .492. He experiences the same types of streaks in hitting that every great player goes through. As Yelich says in the quote, there are times throughout the 162-game Major League Baseball season when his swing feels good and he can hit the ball all over the field. There are, of course, other times in the season when he isn't swinging the bat as well, or things don't quite feel like they should. Ultimately, as a professional, he knows what to do to get back on the right track. **Rating: Cliché City**

Yelich experiences the ups and downs of the long regular season just like any other hitter.

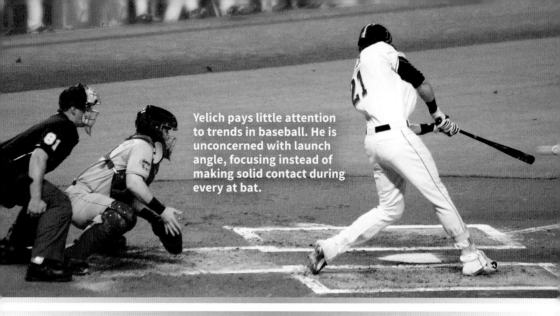

Yelich pays little attention to trends in baseball. He is unconcerned with launch angle, focusing instead of making solid contact during every at bat.

> "I never talked about launch angle, never mentioned launch angle. I know there's a lot of people probably hoping that I would say that because that's just the trend in baseball."

Launch angle is a measurement that baseball analysts use to determine what type of hitter a player is on average. The tool, used mostly to evaluate pitchers, can also determine if a hitter is a low or ground ball hitter or a fly ball hitter. Players who hit the ball on the ground tend to be contact hitters responsible for getting on base with doubles and singles, and fly ball hitters hit more home runs and drive in more runs. It's one of the trends that are used to classify players, but it's not one that Yelich pays much attention to as a player. Hitting home runs and scoring the way he does make him a fly ball hitter with a high launch angle, but he is just as happy simply making contact and advancing a runner. **Rating: Quote Machine**

"I'M GOING TO HIT 50 HOME RUNS!"

Since joining the Brewers, Yelich has hit 72 of his career 131 home runs. This has put him on pace to become one of the game's best power hitters, with a chance to reach 400, 500, or maybe even 600 home runs or more before his career comes to an end. Yelich's ability to hit home runs led him to proclaim, as part of the league's opening day promotional activities, that he would hit 50 homers in the 2019 MLB season. Injuries cost him the chance, as he hit 44 in just 130 games.

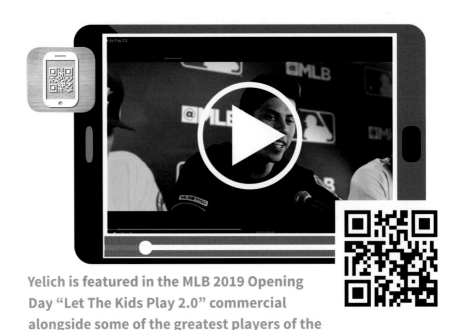

Yelich is featured in the MLB 2019 Opening Day "Let The Kids Play 2.0" commercial alongside some of the greatest players of the game. He proclaimed that he would hit 50 home runs in 2019.

"Any time you can have an impact on anybody's life in a positive direction, to bring happiness to the community or a certain group of people, you don't take that lightly as a team, as a player."

Long before winning the NL MVP award in 2018, Yelich had always made it a point to give back to the community where he played baseball professionally, first in Miami, then Milwaukee. He does not take lightly his job not only as a player and team leader but also as a role model. Yelich's name is not associated with any controversy or gossip as he keeps his head down, eyes focused, and head in the game. This makes him a perfect **ambassador** for the game. Yelich likes the fact that his lead-by-example attitude inspires fans and energizes the community where he plays. Playing baseball is a dream come true for Yelich, and he wants to make his time in the league as fun and inspiring for others as it is for him. **Rating: Quote Machine**

"I had a lot of friends, family friends, that had season tickets, and we'd all go when we were little kids. And you'd go after you played your own baseball game and change out of your uniform in the parking lot of Dodger Stadium to go put on street clothes and go watch the game."

Yelich could easily have been one of the kids in this photo, since he and his friends and family were at Dodger Stadium cheering on Mike Piazza and the team every season when he was growing up.

Yelich grew up in the community of Thousand Oaks, California, which is in the northwest part of the city of Los Angeles. Growing up in Thousand Oaks made him a huge Dodgers fan as a kid. He developed his love for the game by being able to go to see the team play when they were home or following them on the radio or television, in much the same way every kid who grew up loving baseball did. His love for the game and for watching his hometown Dodgers play stayed with him even as he became older, even to the point where he would go straight to Dodgers Stadium from a Little League or high school game, change clothes, and be in the stands ready to cheer on his favorite team.

Rating: Quote Machine

> **"Obviously, you want to bring as much attention to the game as possible and grow baseball as much as you can. It's important. It comes with the responsibility that being a league M.V.P. comes with."**

Winning the MVP Award in 2018 was an awesome accomplishment for Yelich. It also comes with a tremendous amount of responsibility. Part of his responsibility as MVP is to develop in the next generation of players a love and appreciation for the game. Yelich also knows that being MVP invites a great deal of attention, criticism, and a complete examination of every aspect of his life, both on and off the field. He lives his life as a role model and stays away from the temptations that often get other athletes into trouble. Yelich looks to bring only positive attention to himself and, by extension, to the game of baseball. **Rating: Quote Machine**

"**Once you've had success, I think you can go one of two ways. You can either have that success and go downhill, or you can use it to build off of it and continue going upward.**"

Yelich prepares to hit against the Pirates during a 2018 game in Pittsburgh.

This quote is a great summation of how Yelich views his success and what it has the potential to do to a person. Being named MVP and winning several awards after only two years in a Milwaukee Brewers uniform has raised Yelich's profile to that of one of the highest-profile players in MLB. Reaching this level of success can bring with it the potential to negatively affect his life, just as much as it has the potential to take him to places that he could have only imagined before a life in baseball. The trick, as he understands it, is to remain humble, build on the success that he has experienced, and leave the game a shining example to others of what being great means. **Rating: Quote Machine**

> **"If you hit a routine fly ball in the big leagues, you're out every time. If you hit a ground ball, you're probably out a lot of the time as well. But there's a happy medium in there, a way to swing where your misses can still lead to successes."**

Although he does not think much about things like launch angles or the measurements used to determine the type of hitter he is, Yelich understands the science of hitting styles and the theories that surround them. This means that he understands that his success at the plate comes from being somewhere

With three seasons of 20-plus steals under his belt, Yelich has the speed to get around the base paths in a hurry.

in between the type of batter who can get ground balls through the infield and one who hits it up in the air. That "happy medium" between being a ground ball hitter and a fly ball hitter is what helps him reach base consistently and hit home runs when needed to help his team win. Being able to be the type of hitter that is needed in a given situation makes Yelich a feared batter and one of the best in the game. **Rating: Quote Machine**

TEXT-DEPENDENT QUESTIONS

1. What did Yelich say is the biggest thing to focus on?

2. At what event did Yelich announce that he was going to hit 50 home runs in 2019?

3. What team did Yelich cheer for when he was growing up?

 RESEARCH PROJECT

Launch angle is one of the many measurements used by baseball statisticians and analysts to determine the type of pitcher or hitter a player is. Different launch angles determine whether the ball is hit low (ground ball), hard on a line, or in the air (fly ball). Statcast is a baseball statistical tracking service, which tracks launch angles and ranks Yelich among the league's top five hitters based on launch angle data. Compare Yelich's launch angle data for 2018 provided by Statcast to determine the launch angle that produced each of his 36 home runs.

WORDS TO UNDERSTAND

compel: to drive or urge forcefully or irresistibly

insignia: a distinguishing mark or sign

lucrative: producing wealth; profitable

morphed: changed the form or character of; transformed

CHAPTER 5

OFF THE DIAMOND

CHRISTIAN YELICH'S EDUCATION

Yelich attended Westlake High School from 2006–2010, graduating as a senior. He was recruited to play collegiate baseball for the University of Miami Hurricanes. Yelich was intent on attending Miami on an athletic scholarship, but a more **compelling** offer from the Florida Marlins consisting of $1.7 million convinced him to give professional baseball a try instead of college. Yelich turned down the University of Miami's scholarship offer to attend the school in the fall of 2010 and instead joined the Marlins' organization, appearing in a total of 12 games for the team's rookie league club (Gulf Coast Marlins) and Class A team in Greensboro, North Carolina.

YELICH'S HOME AND FAMILY

Yelich, born on December 5, 1991, is the eldest of three sons born to Alecia (mother) and Stephen Yelich Jr. His younger brothers are Collin and Cameron. Collin Yelich, a baseball player in his own right, played for several years between 2013 and 2016 in the Atlanta Braves minor league system as a catcher

Yelich's grandfather, a former NFL halfback, designed the Los Angeles Rams helmet logo.

and first baseman. He last appeared in uniform for the team's Gulf Coast Braves rookie league franchise in August 2016. Yelich has a unique heritage; he is part Serbian and part Japanese. Yelich, who was twenty-seven as of the start of the 2019 MLB season, attributes his youthful appearance to his mother, Alecia, who graduated from high school in 1986 and who herself looks like she could be his older sister.

Yelich comes from a very athletic family that has contributed a lot to the sports history of Los Angeles. Yelich's uncle Chris was an offensive lineman who played for two of the UCLA Bruins Rose Bowl champion teams. Further back, his great-grandfather Fred Gehrke played halfback for the Cleveland and Los Angeles Rams for seven seasons from 1940 to 1950. Gehrke rushed for 1,664 yards (1521.6 m) and 14 touchdowns in his NFL career.

THE INVENTION OF THE TEAM LOGO ON FOOTBALL HELMETS

Fred Gehrke had a very good career playing for the Rams. What he is known for, however, is not his play on the gridiron but for a more permanent, lasting contribution, not only to the team but also to pro football. In the early days of the league, players wore leather helmets as a form of protection from head injury. Over time, the helmets **morphed** into the ones seen in today's NFL. The early helmets had no team **insignia** or logo.

Gehrke was also a graphic arts major at the University of Utah (Nickname: Utes) prior to joining the NFL. He was responsible for coming up with the ram's horn design that has been the insignia of the Los Angeles Rams since 1948. The design of Yelich's grandfather was the first ever to appear on an NFL helmet and became the standard for teams from the 1950s forward. Gehrke is also responsible for the invention of the face mask. The invention came about as a result of him growing tired of having his nose broken as a halfback. The introduction of the painted logo and face mask earned Gehrke an induction into Pro Football's Hall of Fame.

YELICH'S HOMES

Yelich, who is single, makes his home in Milwaukee during the baseball season. Back home, he purchased a $5.6 million house in Malibu, California. The 2,500-square-foot (762-square-meter) home sits on the oceanfront and provides Yelich (and his mom, Alecia—a frequent roommate) great views of the Pacific Ocean. It is the perfect bachelor pad for the young baseball star.

Yelich's offseason home is in the posh Southern California community of Malibu.

HOW YELICH GIVES BACK TO THE COMMUNITY

Yelich sits on the board of advisors for the Taylor Hooton Foundation. The foundation, formed in 2004, is named after a seventeen-year-old athlete who committed suicide, due in part to his use of performance-enhancing steroids. The goal of the organization, formed by Hooton's parents in his memory, is to provide information and support to athletes (and students) in college and high school to make better choices regarding the use of performance-enhancing drugs (PED) and anabolic steroids. Yelich's involvement with the foundation is a natural fit, because he has never given in to the use of PEDs or other drugs.

Yelich is also involved in raising money for victims of violence and natural disasters such as the Woolsey fire that affected residents of Ventura County and Los Angeles in November 2018 (see sidebar).

GOING "CALISTRONG"

Yelich knows that his success on the field is, in part, due to the fans who come out and cheer him on. He owes his development as a player to the days he spent learning the game in his hometown of Thousand Oaks, California, where he grew into a high school star and first-round draft selection of the Florida Marlins. When fires devastated Ventura County and parts of the Greater Los Angeles community where he grew up, Yelich brought together a diverse group of athletes, performers, and others to do what they could to support the victims of the 2018 Woolsey fires.

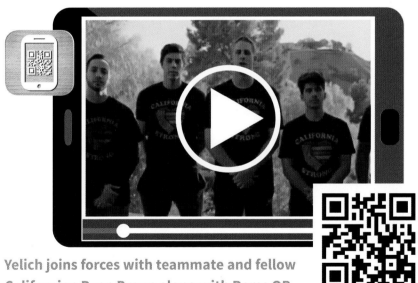

Yelich joins forces with teammate and fellow Californian Ryan Braun along with Rams QB Jared Goff, teammate Mike Moustakas, and others to raise funds and awareness of the plight of victims of the Woolsey fires that devastated homes in the areas where they live.

THE MARKETING OF YELICH

Winning the 2018 NL MVP Award turned out to be very **lucrative** for Yelich. He signed a deal as a celebrity endorser of Sargento Foods Inc. Sargento, based in Plymouth, Wisconsin, produces cheese and other dairy products and is a large corporate sponsor of the Milwaukee Brewers. The deal that Yelich signed with Sargento allows the company to use his image and likeness in the advertising of their products.

Additionally, Yelich has negotiated promotional deals with Pepsi, Chevrolet, a local Wisconsin bank (Associated Bank), and American Family

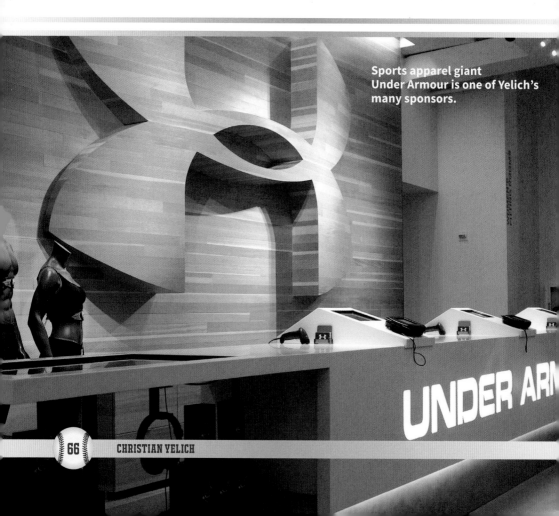

Sports apparel giant Under Armour is one of Yelich's many sponsors.

UNDER ARM

Insurance, a property and casualty insurer based in Madison, Wisconsin. He has also signed deals with the following sports and apparel companies: Under Armour, Stance (socks), New Era, Steiner Sports, Topps, and Louisville Slugger. Yelich's mixed heritage is also helping him find promotional opportunities in Japan. As his star continues to rise, so too will his opportunities to become a bigger sports personality.

SALARY INFORMATION

Sports agent Joseph C. Longo of Paragon Sports International represents Yelich. Longo, who is a licensed attorney, has represented various sports stars over the past three decades. He sits on the agent advisory board for the Major League Baseball Players Association and is an expert in sports negotiations and collective bargaining agreements.

The Florida Marlins signed Yelich in 2010 (after his selection with the 23rd pick in the first round) with a $1,700,000 signing bonus. He spent his first several seasons playing Class A, A+, AAA, and Rookie League ball for the team before becoming a regular player for the Marlins in 2014. His salary doubled from just over $500,000 paid in 2014 to a million dollars and more in 2016 and 2017. Longo negotiated a seven-year contract extension in 2015 for $49.57 million.

Yelich's MVP season has raised his profile around the league to that of a superstar on the rise. His remaining contract with the Brewers (which runs through the 2022 season) will see him earn another $26.5 million before he becomes a free agent at the start of 2022. The team holds an option for that season for $15 million, which will most likely be renegotiated if he turns in a few more MVP-level seasons like the one he had in 2018.

Yelich made slightly more than half a million dollars a year in his first two seasons in Miami.

Yelich's MVP season has raised his profile around the league to that of a superstar on the rise. His remaining contract with the Brewers (which runs through the 2022 season) will see him earn another $26.5 million before he becomes a free agent at the start of 2022. The team holds an option for that season for $15 million, which will most likely be renegotiated if he turns in a few more MVP-level seasons like the one he had in 2018.

Here is a breakdown of Yelich's salary earnings since the 2014 MLB season:

Season	Team (League)	Salary Amount
2014	Miami Marlins (NL)	$ 505,000
2015	Miami Marlins (NL)	$ 570,000
2016	Miami Marlins (NL)	$ 1,000,000
2017	Miami Marlins (NL)	$ 3,500,000
2018	Milwaukee Brewers (NL)	$ 7,000,000
2019	Milwaukee Brewers (NL)	$ 9,750,000
2020	Milwaukee Brewers (NL)	$ 12,500,000
2021	Milwaukee Brewers (NL)	$ 14,000,000
2022	Milwaukee Brewers (NL)	$ 15,000,000*
TOTALS		$ 63,825,000

*The Brewers retain an option for year 2022, Yelich's first year of eligibility for free agency. A team bidding for his services will have to pay the $1.25 million buyout of his contract.

Yelich has always been a promising baseball prospect. From his days at Westlake High School to his stint in the Marlins' minor league system, he has shown flashes of greatness, both in the field and at the plate. A midseason call-up in 2013 gave him the chance to show that he was ready to play in the big leagues. He has proven over his career, especially since being traded to Milwaukee in 2018, that he is destined to become not just a good baseball player but also one of the games' greats. Time will tell, but do not be surprised when Yelich's career is over to find him standing one day next to a bust of his head in Cooperstown, New York. A Hall of Fame induction would show how truly great a career he had (and make him the second Yelich enshrined in a Hall of Fame)!

Yelich's move to Milwaukee has put him on a path to a potential Hall of Fame career.

TEXT-DEPENDENT QUESTIONS

1. How much has Yelich earned in salary in his baseball career (through 2019)?

2. What is his relationship status? In what state(s) does Yelich reside?

3. What foundation is he a member of the board of advisors? What is the mission (purpose) of the foundation?

 RESEARCH PROJECT

Yelich is one of several players affected by tragedies that have happened in or near his hometown. On November 8, 2018, a wildfire ignited in Ventura County (where Thousand Oaks is located) and Los Angeles, burning nearly 97,000 acres of land and killing three people. This event was met with a response from Yelich as he brought teammates and fellow athletes across different sports together to raise money for victims. He is certainly not the only baseball player to contribute his time, money, and efforts in helping the community he grew up in or the one where he lives. Looking at the many recent tragedies over the past 10 years (i.e., natural disasters like floods, hurricanes, and wildfires), name three other players who raised money for victims of these events.

All-Star: a player chosen by fans and managers to play on the All-Star team against the opposing league in the MLB All-Star game in the middle of the season. The league that wins hosts the first game of the World Series.

box: the rectangle where the batter stands or the area where the pitcher fields the ball; also called the batter's box.

breaking ball: any pitch that curves in the air: a curve ball, slider, screwball, sinker, or forkball.

bunt: a ball batted for a short distance to help the batter to reach first base or to advance another runner on base while the defense makes the out at first.

change-up: a slow pitch that throws off a batter's timing.

cleanup: the fourth hitter in the lineup, usually the best hitter on the team. If all three runners get on base before the cleanup hitter, it's up to him to get them home, likely with a home run.

closer: the pitcher called in during the last innings to preserve a lead.

curve: a pitch that spins the ball with a snap of the wrist, forcing it to curve near the plate.

Cy Young Award: the award given annually to the pitcher in each of the American and National Leagues deemed to be the most outstanding in the regular season. The award winner is determined by votes cast by the Baseball Writers' Association of America, a professional association for baseball journalists.

designated hitter (DH): the player who hits for the pitcher. This position was created in 1973 and is used only in the American League.

double play: two outs in one play, for example, a strikeout and a base runner being thrown out, or when two runners are called out on the bases.

doubleheader: when two teams play twice on the same day, one game after the other.

earned run average: ERA is a pitching statistic that measures the average number of earned runs scored against a pitcher for every nine innings pitched.

error: a defensive mistake resulting in a batter reaching base or getting extra bases. The official scorer calls errors.

fastball: a pitch thrown at high speed, usually more than 90 miles per hour (145 km/h) in MLB.

foul ball: when the ball is hit into foul territory. A hitter's first two fouls count as strikes, but a batter can't be called out on a foul ball.

Gold Glove Award: the Gold Glove is given annually to the player at each position in both the American and National Leagues deemed to have exhibited superior fielding performance in the regular season. Votes cast by the team managers and coaches determine the award winner.

grand slam: a home run when runners are on all the bases.

ground-rule double: when a ball is hit fairly but then goes out of play (e.g., over the home run fence after it bounces) but because of an agreed-upon rule for the ball park, the player gets to second base.

hit-and-run: a play in which a base runner runs right when the pitcher pitches, and the hitter tries to hit the ball into play to help the runner get two bases or avoid a double play.

knuckleball: a pitch with as little spin as possible that moves slowly and unpredictably. The pitcher grips the ball with his fingertips or knuckles when throwing the pitch.

line drive: when a batter hits the ball hard and low into the field of play, sometimes called "a rope."

Most Valuable Player Award: the MVP award is given annually to the player in each of the American and National Leagues deemed to be the most valuable to his team in the regular season. The award winner is determined by votes cast by the Baseball Writers' Association of America, a professional association for baseball journalists.

no-hitter: a game in which one team gets no base hits.

pickoff: when a pitcher or catcher throws a runner out, catching him or her standing off the base.

relief pitcher: a pitcher who comes into the game to replace another pitcher.

sacrifice: when a batter makes an out on purpose to advance a runner (e.g., a sacrifice bunt or fly ball). A sacrifice play is not an official at bat for the hitter.

Silver Slugger Award: given annually to the player at each position in each of the American and National Leagues deemed to be the best offensive player in the regular season. Votes cast by the team managers and coaches determine the award winner.

slider: a pitch that is almost as fast as a fastball but curves. The pitcher tries to confuse the batter, who may have trouble deciding what kind of pitch is coming.

stolen base: when a base runner runs right when the pitcher pitches, and if the pitch is not hit, makes it to the next base before being thrown out.

strike zone: the area above home plate where strikes are called. The pitch must be over home plate, above the batter's knees, and below the batter's belt.

strikeout: when a batter gets a third strike, either by missing the ball or not swinging on a pitch that is in the strike zone.

trade deadline: the trade deadline, which typically falls at 4 p.m. ET on July 31, is the last point during the regular season at which players can be traded from one club to another.

walk: when the pitcher throws four pitches outside the strike zone (called balls by the umpire) before throwing three strikes, allowing the hitter to walk to first base.

WAR: this acronym stands for Wins Above Replacement. It is an advanced statistics metric designed to measure the value of a player by indicating how many games a player adds to a team's win total versus those that would be added by the best available replacement player. For position players, the formula is WAR = (Batting Runs + Base Running Runs + Fielding Runs + Positional Adjustment + League Adjustment + Replacement Runs) / (Runs per Win). For pitchers, the formula is WAR = [[([(League "FIP" – "FIP") / Pitcher Specific Runs per Win] + Replacement Level) (IP/9)] Leverage Multiplier for Relievers] + League Correction.

wild pitch: A pitcher is charged with a wild pitch when his pitch is so errant that the catcher is unable to control it, and as a result, the base runner(s) advance.

FURTHER READING

Baseball America. *Baseball America's Before They Were Stars.* Durham, NC: Baseball America, 2019.

Baseball Prospective. *Milwaukee Brewers 2019: A Baseball Companion.* Sterling, VA: Stylus Publishing, LLC, 2019.

Everson, Jeff. *50 Seasons of Milwaukee Brewers Facts*. Scotts Valley, CA: Kindle Direct Publishing, 2019.

Haudicourt, Tom. *Special Brew: An Inside Look at the 2018 Milwaukee Brewers.* Stevens Point, WI: KCI Sports Publishing, 2019.

Lindberg, Ben, and Sawchik, Travis. *The MVP Machine: How Baseball's New Nonconformists Are Using Data to Build Better Players*. New York City: Basic Books, 2019.

INTERNET RESOURCES

https://www.baseball-reference.com/
The baseball-specific resource provided by Sports Reference LLC for current and historical statistics of Christian Yelich.

https://bleacherreport.com/mlb
The official website for Bleacher Report Sport's MLB reports on each of the 30 teams.

https://www.cbssports.com/mlb/teams/MIL/milwaukee-brewers/
The web page for the Milwaukee Brewers provided by CBSSports.com, providing latest news and information, player profiles, scheduling, and standings.

https://www.jsonline.com/sports/brewers/
The web page of the *Milwaukee Journal-Sentinel* newspaper for the Milwaukee Brewers baseball team.

https://www.espn.com/mlb/team/_/name/mil/milwaukee-brewers
The official website of ESPN sports network for the Milwaukee Brewers.

https://www.mlb.com/
The official website of Major League Baseball.

https://www.mlb.com/brewers
The official MLB website for the Milwaukee Brewers baseball team, including history, player information, statistics, and news.

https://sports.yahoo.com/mlb/
The official website of Yahoo! Sports MLB coverage, providing news, statistics, and important information about the association and its 30 teams.

INDEX

INDEX

INDEX

AUTHOR BIOGRAPHY

Donald Parker is an avid sports fan, author, and father. He enjoys watching and participating in many types of sports, including football, basketball, baseball, and golf. He enjoyed a brief career as a punter and defensive back at NCAA Division III Carroll College (now University) in Waukesha, Wisconsin, and spends much of his time now watching and writing about the sports he loves.

PHOTO CREDITS

PHOTO CREDITS

EDUCATIONAL VIDEO LINKS

Chapter 1:

http://x-qr.net/1Jqw

http://x-qr.net/1Lhu

http://x-qr.net/1Kex

http://x-qr.net/1LQ1

http://x-qr.net/1Ko6

http://x-qr.net/1KN1

http://x-qr.net/1Ke0

http://x-qr.net/1LYW

Chapter 2:

http://x-qr.net/1Jvq

Chapter 3:

http://x-qr.net/1K4t

Chapter 4:

http://x-qr.net/1KMn

Chapter 5:

http://x-qr.net/1JoT